RAILWAYS *of the* ISLE OF WIGHT

P. C. ALLEN

AMBERLEY

Front cover and opposite page: Photographs by Gordon Edgar.

First published 2014

Amberley Publishing
The Hill, Stroud
Gloucestershire, GL5 4EP

www.amberley-books.com

Copyright © Amberley Publishing, 2014

The right of Amberley Publishing to be identified
as the Author of this work has been asserted in
accordance with the Copyrights, Designs and
Patents Act 1988.

ISBN 978 1 4456 3784 6 (print)
ISBN 978 1 4456 3796 9 (ebook)

British Library Cataloguing in Publication Data.
A catalogue record for this book is available from
the British Library.

Typesetting by Amberley Publishing.
Printed in the UK.

Contents

Introduction to This Edition

The main text and many of the older photographs for this book come from *The Railways of the Isle of Wight*, written by P. C. Allen and originally published in 1928 by The Locomotive Publishing Company. As the author states in the first section, 'There is probably no place in the British Isles that could offer a more attractive study to one interested in railway working on a small scale than the Isle of Wight'. Indeed, the self-contained nature of an island often produces interesting or idiosyncratic railways, whether it is on the Isle of Man or Reverend Wilbert Awdry's fictional island of Sodor. Curiously, the Isle of Wight is actually England's smallest county when the tide is in, however, when the tide is low it loses that honour to Rutland.

At its height the Island had a network of 55½ miles of line and was operated by a number of independent railway companies, and the 1928 map, shown on page 16, features the Isle of Wight Railway (IWR), the Isle of Wight Central Railway (IWCR), the Freshwater, Yarmouth & Newport Railway (FYNR), as well as the joint lines of the London & South Western Railway (LSWR) and London, Brighton & South Coast Railway (LBSCR). (The LSWR's lines on the mainland are also shown where they come to Stokes Bay and Lymington.) Under the 1923 grouping of Britain's Railways these were amalgamated under the control of the Southern Railway – see sections 3, 4 and 5. P. C. Allen's account covers the years up to 1928 and it is brought up to date with new photo sections at the end of this book.

John Christopher, editor

Opposite: Isle of Wight travel poster, *c.* 1905.

Foreword to the 1928 Edition

To the railway litterateur there must be some unaccountable lure about the railways of the Isle of Wight. I well remember that my own first literary venture was an article describing what I saw on them on a holiday in the Island, and written at the immature age of fourteen; but I was doomed to receive, from the Editor of the railway journal to which I submitted those notes, that widely circulated Editorial letter which begins: 'The Editor regrets ...'

But my friend P. C. Allen (there is no family connection by the way) has been more fortunate. His monograph, describing briefly the history of the Island systems, the effect on them of the railway grouping and the details of their locomotives, will fill a blank, as in the many histories that have been compiled concerning the famous systems of the British mainland, the railways of the Island have been neglected.

I wish the little book every success.

Cecil J. Allen, 29 March 1928

Top: Bembridge station, Isle of Wight Railway, from *All About Our British Railways. (CMcC)*

I

Mainly Historical

There is probably no place in the British Isles that could offer a more attractive study to one interested in railway working on a small scale than the Isle of Wight.

In the first place, in an island, interest is necessarily concentrated and centred and cannot be distracted by contact with other railway systems.

The Island is small enough for the whole of its railway working to be studied thoroughly and easily and yet large enough, with its 58 miles of line, to be an object worthy of interest and to maintain this interest continually.

Before the Railway Grouping of 1923 the three Island systems with their variety of locomotives and rolling stock provided a fascinating study, while the amalgamation of the lines into the Southern Railway has increased, if that were possible, the attractions that the Island held for the railway enthusiast.

The vast improvements in track, locomotives, train service, and rolling stock made since the amalgamation have been fresh sources of interest which could never have been provided by the slender purses of the Island companies.

It is a matter of great regret that since amalgamation so many of the Island locomotives have been withdrawn and sent away to the scrap heap, though it must be confessed that the summer trains were rather beyond their strength, as these little engines had given magnificent service, while their difference of outside appearance gave them all an individuality, which the London & South Western Adams tanks, that have replaced them, most certainly do not possess.

Railway history in the Isle of Wight begins in 1859 when the first Company, the Cowes & Newport Railway, was incorporated.

This line connecting the capital of the Island with the coast, a distance of 4½ miles, presented no superhuman engineering difficulties in construction, though there is a short tunnel just outside Cowes, and being assured of a steady passenger and goods traffic, was financially successful.

The railway was opened in June, 1862, and at that time the station at Newport was a very simple affair, standing where the goods yard is at present, consisting of a single platform with a run round for locomotives.

The Cowes & Newport Railway, some eight years later, built Medina Wharf, near

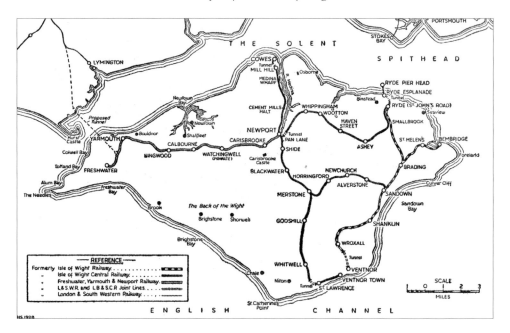

Above: Map of the Island's pre-amalgamation railways, published in P. C. Allen's *The Railways of the Isle of Wight.*

Left: The Isle of Wight photographed by astronaut Chris hadfield on board the International Space Station. *(NASA)*

Below: Railway Clearing House chart of all of the railways on the Island, published in 1914.

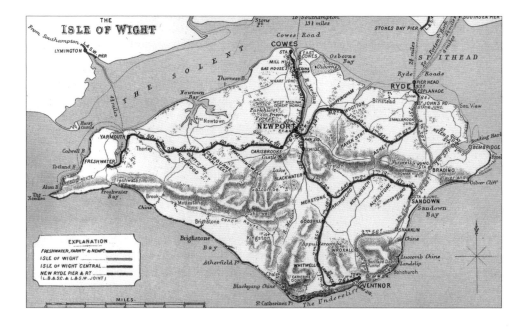

Cowes, which strengthened very much the position of the railway, as it brought the line considerable coal and mineral traffic.

This Company possessed two locomotives for passenger work and a shunting engine for use at Medina Wharf, but these will be dealt with fully later.

The next entry into the field was the Isle of Wight Railway which was incorporated in 1860 and opened, from Ryde, St John's Road, to Shanklin on 23 August, 1864. The cutting of the tunnel three-quarters of a mile in length between Wroxall and Ventnor delayed the opening of the railway to the latter town, 11½ miles from Ryde, until 15 September, 1866.

The local landowners, among them the Earl of Yarborough of that time, offered great opposition to the railway and went out of their way to harass the surveyors.

The intention of the Company was to take the line from Shanklin by Luccumbe, the Landslip and Bonchurch into the town of Ventnor, but the landowners' opposition necessitated a long detour inland by way of Wroxall and under St Boniface Down to a spot considerably above the level of the town, a most awkward situation for a terminus.

During the construction of the tunnel to Ventnor much trouble was encountered with springs; one, however, was unearthed sufficiently robust to supply the town with water, which is conveyed through pipes along the tunnel.

The Isle of Wight Railway was originally authorised as the Isle of Wight Eastern Railway but changed its name when a westward branch was proposed.

This line, connecting Ryde, the chief point of entry to the Island with the holiday resorts of Sandown, Shanklin, and Ventnor was at once a financial success and continued increasingly to be so until the amalgamation of 1923.

The success of these two lines, the Cowes & Newport and the Isle of Wight, encouraged promoters to further efforts of a much less rewarding nature, the subsequent railways being over-capitalized and therefore financial failures.

The next promotion was the Isle of Wight (Newport Junction) Railway, which was authorised in 1868 to construct a line from Sandown to Newport, a distance of 9 miles.

Difficulties with the contractors were experienced and the line was only opened from Sandown to Shide in 1875. It was extended to Pan Lane, Newport, in 1879; the line was, however, a failure, and fell into the hands of the Receiver in that year. In 1880 the IWNJR was extended further into Newport to make junction with the lines already established there.

This railway possessed one decrepit tank engine with an interesting history, and was otherwise worked by the locomotives of the Isle of Wight Railway and by a London & South Western engine hired from Nine Elms.

This line was practically foredoomed to failure from the beginning as, though it started well enough at Sandown at its opening, it ended nowhere in particular, namely at Shide, and did not reach Newport until five years too late.

That the people of Horringford might wish to visit the people of Blackwater was reasonable and proper to suppose, but the Railway Company could not really expect them to do it often enough to make the line pay.

The next undertaking was the Ryde & Newport Railway, which received its Act in 1872, and, after constructional troubles, was opened in December, 1875, the year that the Newport Junction Railway reached Shide.

The line ran from St John's Road, Ryde, for a distance of 8¾ miles to Newport, where a new station was built to accommodate this and the Cowes & Newport Railway.

The track out of Ryde ran parallel with that of the Isle of Wight Railway as far as Smallbrook, a distance of about 1½ miles, giving the appearance of a double line which was in reality two single ones.

On completion, the Ryde & Newport Railway was administered as a joint concern with the Cowes & Newport line, the management being in the hands of a committee appointed by the boards of the two companies.

As has been mentioned, the Isle of Wight (Newport Junction) Railway, although it had already fallen on evil days, had been extended to Newport in 1880, the Receiver therefore gave orders that the Junction Railway be worked by the Joint Committee of the Ryde & Newport and Cowes & Newport Railways. This step paved the way for the amalgamation that took place in 1887 of the three railways, with the formation of the Isle of Wight Central Railway Company.

The first train on the Isle of Wight Railway ready to leave Ryde. The locomotive is the appropriately named *Ryde*, a 2-4-0 built in 1864.

Photochrom view of the pier at Ryde, c. 1900. *(LoC)*

Meanwhile, events were moving in another part of the Island.

Connection between the boats from the mainland at Ryde Pier and the Island railways at St John's Road station had been most inadequately maintained by horse tramway built in 1871; the joint committee of the London & South Western and London, Brighton & South Coast Railways therefore obtained powers to construct a new pier carrying a railway ½ mile out to sea and inland to connect the pier railway to the Island lines at St John's Road. The first part of this undertaking, the line from St John's Road to Esplanade station, which had perforce to tunnel under Ryde Esplanade, was opened on 5 April, 1880, while the line was completed to Pier Head by 12 July of the same year.

The section from Pier Head to St John's Road is worked as a double line and was staffed by the SW&SCR though the traffic was worked by the Island Railways.

The next piece of railway to be opened in the Island was a branch of the Isle of Wight Railway from Brading.

The notorious Liberator Company by reclaiming Brading Harbour from the sea, had turned what had been a prosperous fishing village into a decaying inland hamlet; it was, therefore, possible to build a railway line over the new pasture lands to Bembridge.

Powers had been obtained to make a line to St Helens, when the first part of the IWR was authorised; it was then intended that the line should run along the north side of Brading Harbour to that place. This was the first part of the new branch to be made; the second part from St Helens to Bembridge was then continued close to the new sea wall. This branch, known as the Brading Harbour branch, was opened on 27 May, 1882.

The western end of the Island next claimed the attention of the railway promoter.

In 1872 a railway was proposed under the name of the Freshwater, Bouldnor & Newport Railway; in 1881, however, a line was authorised under the name of the Freshwater, Yarmouth & Newport Railway.

The line was opened for mineral traffic in 1888 and for passenger traffic in 1889 and, from the date of opening until 1913, was worked by the Isle of Wight Central Railway. Under these conditions through trains were run from Ryde to Freshwater, though this journey involves a reversal of the train at Newport as the line from Freshwater does not make a direct approach to Newport station.

In 1913 the directors of the FYNR, dissatisfied with the unreasonable terms on which the IWCR would only consent to work the line, decided that the Company should provide its own motive power and coaching stock. The Central Company retaliated by ordering the Freshwater trains, which had, of course, used the Central station at Newport, to betake themselves elsewhere, so that the FYNR had to build a new station at Newport which involved exasperated passengers in an unnecessary walk of 100 yards between the two.

By 1920, however, an arrangement was come to, by which the Freshwater railway trains could use the bay in the west platform at Newport.

The chief engineering feature of the line is the Town Gate Viaduct, just outside Newport, 576 feet long and 20 feet high.

Ventnor station, from *All About Our British Railways*. *(CMcC)*

Right: Ryde train leaving Ventnor Tunnel. The original 1928 caption reads, 'This photograph shows the polished chimney-cap, dome and handrail in vogue on the IWR twenty-five years ago.'

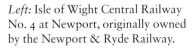

Left: Isle of Wight Central Railway No. 4 at Newport, originally owned by the Newport & Ryde Railway.

Below: IWCR No. 5 at Newport. This locomotive was built for the N&RR.

Shanklin, IWR in Southern Railway colours outside Ryde Shed.

The *Ryde* repaired and fitted with LSWR-type chimney at Brading.

No. W15, *Ventnor*, scrapped after over a million miles on the Island.

The last section of line to be constructed in the Isle of Wight was the Newport, Godshill and St Lawrence Railway, built with the intention of providing a direct route from Newport to Ventnor.

The line was opened from Merstone, on the Newport–Sandown line, to St Lawrence in 1897, and thence to Ventnor Town station in 1900. This line, though a separate undertaking, was worked by the Central Railway from its opening until 1913 when the Receiver, an officer who, unfortunately, has played all too large a part in railway history in the Island, decided that it should be absorbed into the Central Company.

This section of the Central Railway provides one of the finest views in the Island as the line, on emerging from the tunnel between Whitwell and St Lawrence, is carried sharply downhill on the side of a ledge on the hillside high above the undercliff and the English Channel.

This completes the history of actual railway construction in the Island, leaving the three Companies, the Isle of Wight Railway, the Isle of Wight Central Railway, and the Freshwater, Yarmouth & Newport Railway in control of all the Island traffic, though if the ideas of the railway promoters had been fulfilled many more miles of track would have been opened.

First of all, the Isle of Wight Railway proposed building a branch from Wroxall to Newport, this proposal causing the change of name of the Company from the Isle of Wight Eastern Railway to the Isle of Wight Railway.

The IWR did, however, gain access to the centre of the Island when the Isle of Wight (Newport Junction) line from Sandown was opened as they had a share in the working of the line, and would have been well advised to obtain entire control of it when the Company came to grief. For the Isle of Wight Railway, by their application to the Railway Commissioners in 1888 to secure equal rates for the longer journey from Ryde to Newport via Sandown, showed how much they valued the traffic of this line.

In 1874 a proposal was made to build the Ventnor & Yarmouth Railway, along what is known as the Back of the Wight, a district which to this day is without railway service.

Other proposals were the Shanklin & Chale Railway and the Ashey & Horringford Railway, this latter an ambitious scheme as it meant circumventing or tunnelling under Ashey down and Arreton down.

Finally there was the South Western & Isle of Wight Junction Railway scheme to construct a tunnel under the Solent from the Lymington branch of the London & South Western Railway to the Freshwater, Yarmouth & Newport Railway between Freshwater and Yarmouth. This idea had, perforce, to be abandoned during the War.

Proposals were also considered to continue the FYNR beyond Freshwater to the holiday resort of Todand Bay which then and now is only reached by LSWR steamers and by road.

Administration Before Amalgamation

In a clear understanding of the problems that confronted the Island Railways before amalgamation in their efforts to prosper, the steamship routes from the Isle of Wight to the mainland, illustrated in the map on page 8 are the chief factors.

The routes in operation were three, first that worked by the London & South Western and London, Brighton & South Coast Joint steamers, from Portsmouth to Ryde via Southsea, second the London & South Western route from Lymington to Yarmouth and Totland Bay, and lastly the Southampton–Cowes line of boats worked by the Southampton, Isle of Wight, & South of England Royal Mail Steam Packet Co.

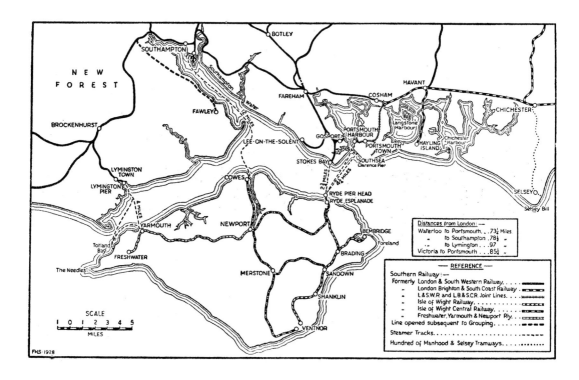

Beyer & Peacock tank engine, No. 8 of the IWCR.

Another route from Stokes Bay to Ryde run by the LSWR was abandoned before the War, though this actually provided the shortest sea crossing of 2¾ miles.

The aim of the Island railways was, of course, to secure as large a share of the summer tourist traffic as they could, which was the very life blood of their systems.

While the Isle of Wight Railway, with its main line from Ryde to Ventnor via Sandown and Shanklin, was in a secure position, the Isle of Wight Central Railway was otherwise placed, and the situation of the Freshwater, Yarmouth & Newport Railway without a single large town on the line, except its terminus, was of necessity precarious.

The Isle of Wight Central Railway had therefore to point out to travellers that the most obvious route to certain points in the Island was not necessarily the best.

Thus while it would seem clear that the best way to reach Yarmouth, Freshwater and Western Wight is by Lymington, the Central Railway aided by the Brighton & South Coast Railway showed it to be otherwise, and persuaded tourists to travel by Portsmouth, Ryde and Newport via the Central and Freshwater Railways, running through trains from Ryde to Freshwater until 1913, when the severance of the FYNR prevented this.

In the same way, in order to capture some of the Isle of Wight Railway traffic to Sandown and Ventnor the Central Railway advertised successfully the route by Southampton, Cowes and Newport.

These efforts on the part of the Isle of Wight Central Railway to increase their passenger traffic though remunerative did little to shake the position of the Isle of Wight Railway which after all possessed the most direct route to the holiday side of the Island, as is shown by figures taken from the Island time tables of the 1924 summer services.

The time taken from London to Sandown by Ryde and Portsmouth is 3 hours 18 minutes by the best trains as compared with 4 hours 6 minutes by the Southampton–Cowes route.

No. 6, Isle of Wight Central Railway 4-4-0, built 1890.

The times from Ventnor are, by the two routes, respectively 3 hours 48 minutes and 4 hours 12 minutes. From Freshwater the best service of coach, steamer and rail via Lymington does the journey in 3½ hours, while the Isle of Wight overland route via Ryde requires 25 minutes longer.

While the Isle of Wight Central Railway never secured such a passenger traffic as its rival the Isle of Wight Railway enjoyed, the boot was on the other leg when it came to goods traffic.

This was chiefly due to the possession of Medina Wharf, which is the point of arrival of nearly all the coal that comes into the Island, colliers up to 1,000 tons being dealt with there.

The Isle of Wight Railway also owned a wharf at St Helens, but this never attracted as much traffic as Medina Wharf owing to uncertainties of navigation of the harbour.

The cement mills on the Central Railway, near Newport, also provided traffic in the transport of chalk from the quarries at Shide and of the cement itself.

Passenger traffic was much increased in the Isle of Wight when, just before the War, passengers were carried on all trains at the normal third-class rate of a penny a mile, as, previously, only a few trains had carried third-class passengers, though cheap tickets had been freely issued.

Though the Island lines were single throughout, a portion of the old IWR main line having been recently doubled, a good service of trains was run owing to frequent crossing loops. These were provided at Brading, Sandown and Shanklin on the IWR; at Ashey, Whippingham, Merstone and Whitwell on the IWCR, and at Ningwood and Yarmouth on the Freshwater line. The Isle of Wight Railway ran an hourly service between Ryde and Ventnor, while the Central line provided an hourly service between Newport and Cowes, Ryde and Sandown in the summer. The services on the Bembridge, Ventnor Town and Freshwater lines were, of course, less frequent; in addition, the post-war train service on most sections of the Island railways was inferior to the pre-war, though such a falling off was not confined to the Isle of Wight.

Since the amalgamation the train services have been much improved as will be shown by the figures appearing later.

The times allowed for the trains to do the various journeys are as follows: Ryde Pier Head to Ventnor, 12½ miles, 45 minutes; Newport to Ryde Pier Head, 10 miles, 30 minutes; Newport to Sandown, 9 miles, 26 minutes; Newport to Freshwater, 12 miles, 34 minutes.

These times would appear to be on the generous side, but it must be remembered that there are frequent stops and heavy gradients to be encountered, and, on the Isle of Wight Railway at least, quantities of luggage to be dealt with; there are also speed limits to be observed, the maximum allowed at any time being 40 miles an hour, though in the old days the drivers may not always have been too attentive to this particular restriction.

The severity of the gradients imposes a lot of hard work on the Island locomotives and some gradient figures may, therefore, be of interest.

On the Isle of Wight Railway the line is only 9 feet above sea level between Brading and Sandown yet 6½ miles further on, at the mouth of the Ventnor tunnel, the line has risen 300 feet; in this section of the line is the famous Apse bank between Shanklin and

Train leaving Sandown station, Isle of Wight Railway. *(CMcC)*

Wroxall where the line rises steadily for nearly 3 miles of 1 in 70. On the other lines gradients are even more severe. Between Ryde and Newport, on the Central line, there are stretches of 1 in 61 each side of Wootton, while between Whitwell and St Lawrence there are 1¾ miles of 1 in 55 falling towards St Lawrence, and sections of 1 in 55 and 1 in 56 between St Lawrence and Ventnor Town.

The steepest grade on the IWCR is, however, between Alverstone and Sandown where the line rises for half a mile of 1 in 54 into Sandown Junction.

On the Freshwater, Yarmouth & Newport Railway 1 in 66 is common and there are stretches of 1 in 63 between Ningwood and Calboume, near Watchingwell private station, and between Carisbrook and Newport, while 1 in 64 is found at Wellow siding near Yarmouth and between Calboume and Watchingwell. The most severe gradient in the whole Island is, however, on the SW and SCR joint metals, as this line had to make a very sudden drop in order to negotiate Ryde Esplanade, so that a descent of 1 in 50 is made from Ryde Esplanade station to the mouth of the tunnel.

The railways, even with these generous schedules, had an ill-deserved reputation for bad time keeping, but any fault in this direction could usually be traced to the mainland.

For in nearly every case the departure times of Island trains were dependent on the boats, which, in turn, were delayed by late arrivals of the mainland trains, consequently an error of a few minutes of a train's arrival at Portsmouth upset all the Island connections as far as Freshwater, trains often being due to leave there before they had arrived!

On the Isle of Wight Railway the late running of a train in one direction did not affect adversely the running of trains on the other direction nearly so much as on those branches where a shuttle service was the rule, as it was possible to arrange for trains to cross at stations nearer the point of late departure than Sandown, the usual crossing place.

Thus, if a train left Ryde Pier Head five minutes late, it would cross the Up train at Brading, so as not to hold the latter up unnecessarily at Sandown.

Throughout the Island, however, when trains ran independent of the boats, excellent time keeping was always the rule.

In other departments, such as track, locomotives, stock, etc., it must be admitted that the railways just prior to the amalgamation were none too well served. Thus the track of the Central and Freshwater railways consisting largely of 70 lbs spiked down rails was in poor order and, while the track of the Isle of Wight Railway consisting of 95 lbs chaired rails was better, this latter system was manifestly short of locomotives.

On the Central Railway a locomotive shortage was not so noticeable, though some engines were getting rather old and replacements were desirable.

It may be safely said, therefore, that the Railways of the Island were ripe for amalgamation and were likely to prove assets to the Southern system, provided certain reforms and improvements, which the Island companies could hardly be expected to undertake with their small resources, were carried out.

In the next chapter it will be shown how completely and how rapidly the Southern Railway has done this, with the result that railway working in the Island has been immensely improved.

No. 8 of the IWCR repainted in Southern Railway's green, photographed at Newport.

No. 12 of the Isle of Wight Central Railway, one of the original Stroudley 'Terriers'.

No. 7, IWCR, originally owned by the Midland & South Western Junction Railway.

Left: No. 7, IWCR, originally owned by the Midland & South Western Junction Railway.

Below: No. 3, IWCR as modified for rail-motor service.

Left: No. 11, Isle of Wight Central Railway. This was the famous 'Terrier' No. 40 *Brighton*.

3

The Coming of the Southern Railway

At the end of 1922 there were five separate railway undertakings in the Island, the three Island railways, the lines of the SW&SCR between Ryde Pier Head and St John's Road, and the LSWR depot at Yarmouth Pier.

In accordance with the Railway Act of 1921, the Isle of Wight and the Isle of Wight Central Railways amalgamated voluntarily and became part of the Southern system as from 1 January, 1923; the Freshwater, Yarmouth & Newport Railway did not acquiesce to this arrangement and was compulsorily included in the Southern Railway on 1 August, 1923.

Immediately on amalgamation the Southern Company set about the improvement of the Island railway facilities.

It was at once realised that a half-hour service between Ryde and Ventnor for the summer was a necessity for increase in passenger traffic and this could only be brought about by the provision of a crossing loop at Wroxall, a station that in the pre-amalgamation days had only one platform, albeit a refreshment room, the only one on the Isle of Wight system.

This work was put in hand at once and the loop was open early in 1924 and enabled a half-hour summer service to be run that year.

The Southern Railway also set about re-building the station at Ryde Pier Head, which was an out of date wooden structure and replacing it with a more modern building. The stations at Sandown, Shanklin, Ventnor and Freshwater have also been improved.

It was realised that, even with such crossing loops as existed, efficient running of trains on the IWR section was not possible as long as the Up trains were delayed by the late Down trains, so that work was put in hand to alleviate this.

The double single line from Ryde St John's to Smallbrook was converted into a true double line by providing a junction at Smallbrook whence two single lines to Brading and Ashey diverged.

This provision made it no longer necessary for trains to wait at Brading and St John's Road until they obtained the staff from trains crossing them; this junction was open by the autumn of 1926.

Soon after work had been started at Smallbrook, another section, between Brading and Sandown, was undertaken, the Company having decided to double the track between those points. Considerable work was involved in this, as several bridges had to be replaced, but the new section was open for traffic on 23 June, 1927, and saved delay for trains at Sandown.

During the last year (1927) ground has also been prepared for continuation of the double track to Shanklin, though not in the direction of Ryde, to link up with the Up and Down lines at Smallbrook.

It is clear that the intention of the Southern Railway is to double the whole of the IWR main line, at any rate from Ryde to Wroxall, though it is unlikely that it would ever be worth the expense of cutting another tunnel through St Boniface Down to Ventnor, the present tunnel only having provision for a single track.

On the Central Railway, reforms were also proceeding though they were less momentous. Such track as was in poor repair was replaced by chaired rails, though spiked down rails are still to be seen in Newport station and yard and on the Ventnor branch; incidentally Ventnor Town station was at once renamed Ventnor West. The Adams tanks brought over to the Island are sometimes derailed in Newport yard as their greater weight (nearly 47 tons) forces the old rails apart so that track replacements there are a necessity.

The Southern Railway also introduced a half-hourly service between Cowes and Newport by altering the time table so that trains arrived at Newport from Ryde and Sandown at an interval of half an hour, whereas under the Central regime with an hourly service to Cowes, trains from Ryde and Sandown arrived at Newport at the same time, one of them going on to Cowes and the other making Newport its terminus.

Between Ryde and Newport, crossing loops existed at Ashey and Whippingham, but these were too near the termini of Newport and Ryde for convenience, so that the Southern Railway abandoned these and rebuilt the station at Haven Street with an island platform, so that trains could be conveniently crossed on the Ryde–Newport branch; the new station was opened in 1926.

Through trains from Newport to Ventnor West were discontinued, better facilities being provided by a shuttle-service from Merstone to Ventnor, connecting with Newport–Sandown trains; this branch is worked by a push-and-pull train in winter and an ordinary train in summer.

Certain through train services on the Central Section were introduced, though the Ryde–Freshwater service was not restored.

A few trains now run through from Sandown to Freshwater with a change of locomotives at Newport, while on Sundays trains run from Cowes and Newport to Shanklin, via Sandown.

The locomotive shops of the Central and Freshwater lines at Newport were abandoned by the Southern Railway, all repairs now being done at the old IWR shops at Ryde St John's.

On the Freshwater branch track relaying was undertaken between Freshwater and Yarmouth while the two viaducts on the system, at Newport and Calbourne, were strengthened so that the speed restrictions in force on them could be abolished.

The crossing loop at Ningwood was also brought into use so that an improved summer service could be run, while the wooden platform at Newport was demolished.

The vast improvements brought about in train service can be best seen by means of the following table:

Route	1913 (Winter)		1919–22 (Winter)		1926 (Winter)		1927 (Summer)	
	Weekday	Sunday	Weekday	Sunday	Weekday	Sunday	Weekday	Sunday
Ryde–Ventnor	13*	6	10	4	15	9	23**	10
Newport–Cowes	12	7	12	7	25	9	25	10
Newport–Ryde	8	6	8	6	14	6	15	8
Newport–Sandown	8	3	6	3	8	6	14	6
Merstone–Ventnor	7	2	5	2	6	0	10	0
Newport–Freshwater	6	4	5	2	7	4	10	5

* 17 in Summer.   ** 26 on Saturdays.
This list does not include trains that run on special days.

The figures speak for themselves and show what is being done to combat the motorbus services, a menace to the Island lines which has been steadily growing since the Armistice.

The introduction of cheap return tickets, however, available for day of issue, has brought a tremendous increase in summer traffic, as shown by the increase in the number of summer trains, which can now be handled with the additional locomotives and rolling stock available.

It might be argued that these cheap return tickets should have been started years ago, but, much as the Island railways would have welcomed additional passenger traffic, they could never have undertaken the capital cost of providing so much new stock and the running expenses of so many additional trains.

These cheap tickets are available daily, enabling a return journey to be made at the price of a single ticket, undercutting the motor 'bus fares considerably, and have been deservedly successful.

The incursion of the Southern Railway into the Island provided many strange sights, interesting to the railway observer.

Almost at once new coaches appeared in the Island painted in the Southern green, while two Adams tanks, still in LSWR colours were brought over in 1923 to relieve the pressure on the IWR main line.

The locomotives of the Island railways in their old livery ran to all parts of the compass without regard to the limits of the old systems.

Isle of Wight Railway engines, still in the well known red, hauled trains into Newport, while Central locomotives were shedded at Ryde.

One of the Freshwater engines went to Medina Wharf, while pre-war days were recalled when Central locomotives again headed the Freshwater trains.

The only combination not recorded is that of an Isle of Wight Railway locomotive on the Freshwater branch, though a double-headed train has been seen running into Newport from Cowes with an IWR and a Central engine in charge.

No. 2, IWCR, originally built for the Marquess of Londonderry's Railway.

Soon the locomotives and stock reappeared overhauled and repainted in the Southern green, more and more coaches and train sets came over from the mainland and additional Adams tanks, already repainted at Eastleigh, were sent across.

Then came the unhappy day when it was found that some of the old Island locomotives were unfit for further work, most of them having insufficient power to deal with the heavier trains, while some developed defects that were not worth the expense of repair.

In 1923 the *Sandown*, one of the original Isle of Wight Railway locomotives, was removed to Eastleigh for scrapping after 59 years' service, without even being numbered under the new scheme that came into force. In July, 1925, the *Ventnor*, which had been repainted and given a number went the same way; in her 57 years' work in the Island this engine covered no fewer than 1,348,548 miles, chiefly on the 12½ miles between Ryde Pier Head and Ventnor. Other Island locomotives have unfortunately disappeared, never to return, but against this may be set the fact that the IWR engine, *Ryde*, built in 1864, is still going well, despite her 63 years of age and a new and hideous disfigurement in the shape of an LSWR chimney; she is, indeed, the oldest passenger locomotive in daily service in Great Britain.

It will be a thousand pities if the Southern Railway ever allow this splendid old engine to be broken up, for the *Ryde* is deserving of preservation, if not as an example of engineering practice, at any rate as a worthy specimen of British workmanship.

As to the future of railway development in the Island, it is probable that further improvements will be of a conventional character. Thus the next few years will see the doubling of the old IWR main line right down to Wroxall and other parts of the system whose traffic warrant it, such as the line from Newport to Cowes, though doubling of this section would involve rebuilding the short tunnel at Mill Hill; the Newport–Ryde section might in time develop sufficient traffic to make the capital cost worth considering.

The trailing connection that the Freshwater branch makes with the old Central line north of Newport is most inconvenient as it requires reversal for Freshwater line trains to enter Newport station. And it is clear that direct access for the Freshwater branch to Newport would be desirable, though difficult to accomplish owing to sidings occupying the ground where a new line would have to be constructed.

The word electrification has often been heard of in connection with the Island Railways, but, though this would result in accelerated and economical services, it is very unlikely that the traffic would increase to such an extent that it would justify the enormous capital outlay, particularly as there is still scope for improved steam-train services.

For the same reason the future will probably see no further mileage of track opened.

The Solent tunnel scheme is another that would profoundly modify the railway character of the Island, but at present it seems as far, or further off, than ever.

Considerable track improvements on the Freshwater and Ventnor West branches are to be expected and a general strengthening of bridges, should increased traffic demand faster, heavier trains with more powerful engines.

The Adams tanks imported from the LSWR are fully up to the work imposed on them but, unfortunately, the future will assuredly see the removal of all the old Island engines with the exception of the six-coupled tanks which are useful for shunting, goods and branch line work.

Brading station. *All About Our British Railways.* (CMcC)

Ryde, with the last type of IWR chimney, at Ventnor.

Ventnor, Isle of Wight Railway, on old turntable points at Ventnor.

IWR *Bonchurch* at Ventnor, St Boniface Down is visible in the background.

4

The Locomotives

The Isle of Wight Central Railway

This railway, as has been mentioned, was the product of the amalgamation of three lines, the Cowes & Newport, the Newport & Ryde, and the Isle of Wight (Newport Junction), it therefore had a very heterogeneous stock of locomotives with which to begin its career in 1887.

The Cowes & Newport Railway started work with two outside cylinder 2-2-2 well tanks named *Pioneer* and *Precursor*; these were built by Slaughter, Gruning & Co., of Bristol, in 1861, the makers' numbers being 453 and 454, and had first been used by the contractors making the line.

When at work on the C&NR these locomotives were painted light blue, lined with red, but on becoming the property of the Central Railway, they were repainted in the dark red, at that time the standard colours of the IWCR, and numbered 1 and 2.

The Central Company also fitted sandboxes on top of the boiler as the original ones were inadequate, and removed the names. These locomotives were scrapped in 1904.

The leading dimensions were:

Cylinders (outside), 13½ inches by 16 inches
Wheels, driving, 5 feet 0 inches, leading and trailing, 3 feet 2 inches
Heating surface, 549 sq. ft
Boiler pressure, 120 lbs per sq. in.
Capacity, water, 400 gallons; coal, 6 cwt
Weight in working order, 19 tons 5 cwt

On the completion of Medina Wharf in 1870 the Cowes & Newport Railway purchased a small front coupled saddle tank for use there, and this engine became No. 3 on the Central Railway. This locomotive was built in 1870 by Black, Hawthorn & Co. (Works No. 116) of Gateshead-on-Tyne, and worked for many years at the Wharf. About 1907, however, the Central Railway bought from the Midland Railway a 12-wheel bogie coach to be used with a small engine as a relief for the rail-motor, then in use.

The first locomotive on the Island, old No. 1 of the Isle of Wight Central Railway, originally named *Pioneer*.

No. 3 worked in this manner until 1913 when the rail-motor service was abandoned; for these duties the appearance of No. 3 underwent some changes; a large cab covering the firebox and bunker replaced the old small cab and the copper-capped chimney was replaced by a cast-iron one on a slightly extended smoke box; a Westinghouse brake was also fitted.

The new cab gave the engine a most grotesque appearance. Originally No. 3 was painted olive green on the Cowes line but later wore the standard colours of the Central system.

Leading dimensions:

Cylinders (outside), 10 inches by 17 inches
Wheels, coupled, 3 feet 3 inches, trailing, 2 feet 4 inches
Heating surface, 304 sq. ft
Boiler pressure, 140 lbs per sq. in.
Capacity, water, 400 gallons; coal, 28 cu. ft
Weight in working order, 15½ tons.

This locomotive was sold in January, 1918, to Holloway Bros, of London, for use on the dock extension of Furness, Withy & Co., at Middlesbrough.

Two locomotives had been built in 1876 for the Newport & Ryde Railway and these became Nos 4 and 5 of the Central Company. They were 2-4-0 inside cylinder side tanks built by Beyer, Peacock & Co., of Manchester (Works Nos 1583 and 1584) and were named *Cowes* and *Osborne*. When they first became the property of the IWCR they were very handsome machines with copper-topped chimneys, polished brass domes and red paint, but the livery of the Central Railway was changed to a sombre black some years before the war so that their appearance suffered.

The brass domes were painted over during the War and No. 5 was given the IWCR standard cast-iron chimney and new cab wings at the same time. No. 4 retained its old copper topped chimney, painted over, until just before the amalgamation into the Southern Railway when it became like No. 5 in appearance.

Leading dimensions of Nos 4 and 5:

Cylinders (inside), 14 inches by 20 inches
Wheels, coupled, 5 feet; leading, 3 feet 3 inches
Heating surface, 605 sq. ft
Boiler pressure, 120 lbs per sq. in.
Capacity, water, 480 gallons; coal, 15 cwt
Weight in working order, 26 tons 8 cwt

The original No. 6 of the Isle of Wight Central Company was the sole locomotive contribution of the Isle of Wight (Newport Junction) Railway.

This line was worked by this No. 6 and by the Isle of Wight Railway, in turn with one of the Beattie 2-4-0 tanks of the LSWR, No. 36, *Comet*, hired under onerous terms.

Old No. 6 was a 2-2-2 inside cylinder well tank with outside frames, built in 1861 by R. & W. Hawthorn (Works No. 1128) for the Whitehaven Junction Railway.

No. 5, a 2-4-0 built in 1876 for the IWCR. Renumbered as W5, scrapped in August 1926.

It then came into the hands of the Joint Committee of the Whitehaven Junction and Whitehaven & Furness Junction Railways, whose locomotive stocks were combined; the Joint Committee named the engine *Queen Mab*. In 1866 the parts of the Joint Committee were amalgamated with the Furness and London & North Western Railways, the locomotives being divided between these two.

The *Queen Mab* became the property of the Furness Railway by whom it was numbered 46. The Furness Company sold it to the IWNJR in 1875, and the latter named it *Newport*. It eventually became No. 6 of the IWCR in 1887, but was on the duplicate list by 1890 and scrapped in 1895.

No. 6 had 5-foot-6-inch driving wheels and cylinders 14 inches by 20 inches.

The next locomotive in service was purchased in 1880 by the Ryde, Cowes and Newport Joint Committee from the North London Railway.

This was a 4-4-0 inside cylinder side tank, with a cast-iron chimney and a polished brass dome with spring balance safety valves, built in 1861 by Slaughter, Gruning & Co. (Makers' No. 443). In the hands of the North London Railway it had been numbered 35 and 106, and became No. 7 of the IWCR. It was scrapped in 1906.

Principal dimensions:

Cylinders (inside), 15½ inches by 22 inches
Wheels, coupled, 5 feet 3 inches; bogie, 3 feet 2 inches
Heating Surface, 969 sq. ft
Boiler pressure, 120 lbs per sq. in.
Capacity, water, 800 gallons; coal, 14 cwt
Weight in working order, 34½ tons

In 1890 the Isle of Wight Central Railway ordered from Black, Hawthorn & Co., a 4-4-0 outside cylinder side tank for heavy passenger work. This locomotive (Works No. 999) became the new No. 6 of the Central Railway.

From the time of its delivery to its absorption into the locomotive stock of the Southern Railway it underwent few changes, being given the IWCR standard chimney and the Westinghouse brake.

Leading dimensions:

Cylinders (outside), 16 inches by 22 inches
Wheels, coupled, 5 feet 3 inches; bogie, 3 feet
Heating surface, 880 sq. ft
Boiler pressure, 140 lbs per sq. in.
Capacity, water, 700 gallons; coal, 45 cu. ft
Weight in working order, 40 tons

In 1898 another engine was ordered for the Central line, this time from Beyer, Peacock & Co. (Works No. 3942), and was a slightly enlarged edition of Nos 4 and 5.

Thus leading and driving wheels were an inch larger in diameter while the working pressure was increased to 150 lbs per sq. in.; 40 gallons more water could be carried and 1 cwt more coal could be disposed of in an outside bunker; the weight in working order was thus increased to 30 tons 16 cwt.

When the black livery was introduced, No. 8, as this engine was numbered, had the brass dome painted over while the copper-capped chimney was changed for the IWCR cast-iron type.

This locomotive arrived in the Island in May, 1898, and from that moment ran 1,050 miles a week for 27 weeks on end, without being withdrawn for a single day.

March, 1899, saw the purchase of another engine, which became No. 9, one of the LB&SCR Stroudley 'Terriers', originally No. 74, *Shadwell*, which was built in 1872.

In April, 1900, another 'Terrier', No. 69, *Peckham*, built in 1874, was bought from the LB&SCR and became IWCR No. 10; while in January, 1902, the famous 'Terrier' No. 40, *Brighton*, built in 1878, which had gained a gold medal at the Paris Exhibition of that year, was sold to the Central Railway and became No. 11.

Eventually a fourth of these useful engines was added to the Central lists as No. 12 in November, 1903, ex No. 84, *Crowborough*, of 1880.

The leading dimensions of this famous class are:

Cylinders (inside), 14 inches by 20 inches
Wheels, 4-foot diameter
Heating surface, *Nos 9 and 10*, 518 sq. ft; *Nos 11 and 12*, 510 sq. ft space
Boiler pressure, 140 lbs per sq. in.
Capacity, water, 500 gallons; coal, 1 ton
Weight in working order, 24 tons 7 cwt

The bunkers of these engines were all enlarged by the Central Company and the tool boxes dispensed with. New boilers for an increase of pressure up to 150 lbs were fitted and injectors in place of pumps.

Cast-iron chimneys, of slightly different patterns, replaced the copper-capped chimneys which were the standard Brighton practice.

In 1906 a steam rail-motor was ordered from R. & W. Hawthorn, Leslie & Co. (Makers' No. 2669), the feature being that the engine and coach portions were distinct.

The locomotive was an outside cylinder 0-4-0 side tank, and was numbered 1 in the place of the old Cowes and Newport engine.

The rail-motor was not a success, so that the trailer portion was converted into an ordinary coach while No. 1 after carrying out some shunting duties was sold in 1918 to the same purchasers as No. 3.

Its dimensions were:

Cylinders (outside), 9 inches by 14 inches
Wheels, 3 feet 6 inches
Heating surface, 329 sq. ft
Capacity, water, 400 gallons; coal, 12 cwt
Weight of engine portion, 15½ tons

In 1908 a 2-4-0 inside cylinder tank engine was bought from the Midland & South Western Junction Railway to replace old No. 7, the North London tank which had been scrapped.

This engine was also numbered 7, and was built by Beyer, Peacock & Co. in 1882 (Makers' No. 2231), being similar to Nos 4, 5 and 8 though considerably more powerful.

Its figures were:

Cylinders (inside), 16 inches by 24 inches
Wheels, coupled, 5 feet 6 inches; leading, 4 feet
Heating surface, 952 sq. ft
Boiler pressure, 140 lbs per sq. in.
Capacity, water, 1,000 gallons; coal, 1 ton
Weight in working order, 35 tons

This locomotive was numbered 6 on the MSWJR and ran on the Central with a copper-capped chimney and a polished brass dome with spring balance safety valves.

The chimney was replaced by a cast-iron one and the dome painted over, while in 1920 the spring balances were removed, the chimney shortened by 5 inches, and Ramsbottom safety valves fitted.

The last engine obtained by the Isle of Wight Central Railway was a 0-4-4 inside cylinder side tank bought from the North Eastern Railway in 1909. This locomotive was built at Seaham in 1895 for the Marquis of Londonderry's Railway and was numbered 21; when the Seaham Harbour Railway was taken over by the North Eastern in 1900, it was numbered 1712, and finally became No. 2 IWCR.

It had long side tanks reaching to the front of the driving wheels on arrival, but these were cut down and at the same time a cast-iron chimney and the Westinghouse brake were fitted.

This locomotive proved unsatisfactorily heavy and was sold in July, 1917, to Armstrong, Whitworth & Co., of Elswick.

The leading dimensions of No. 2 were:

Cylinders (inside), 17 inches by 24 inches
Wheels, coupled, 5 feet 4½ inches; trailing, 3 feet
Heating surface, 895 sq. ft
Boiler pressure, 130 lbs per sq. in.
Capacity, water (reduced), 600 gallons
Weight in working order, 45 tons 17 cwt

The engines for some years prior to amalgamation were painted black with red and white lines and red buffer beams, and lettered I.W.C. on the tank sides. Nos 7 and 8 had red connecting rods.

The engines also carried destination boards, white letters on a red ground, on the bunker or at the base of the chimney.

Ventnor, Isle of Wight Railway.

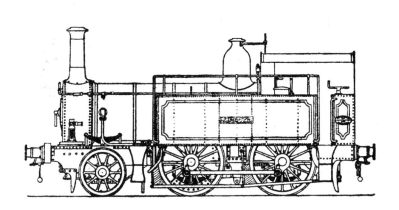

IWR *Sandown*, with the original boiler.

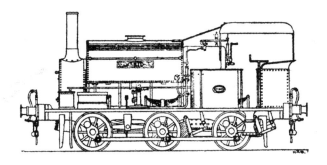

The *Bembridge* after alterations made by the IWR.

The locomotives, with the exception of the six-coupled tanks, were fitted with hooters instead of ordinary whistles, while the 'Terriers' were conventional in this respect.

Locomotives on the Central System usually run bunker first towards Cowes.

The Isle of Wight Railway

When the Isle of Wight Railway was opened in 1864, the Company had just acquired three 2-4-0 inside cylinder side tanks from Beyer, Peacock & Co. (Works' Nos 400, 401, 402) named *Ryde*, *Sandown* and *Shanklin*, which were built in that year.

These locomotives were identical and had the following leading dimensions:

Cylinders (inside), 15 inches by 20 inches
Wheels, coupled, 5 feet; leading, 3 feet 6 inches
Heating surface, 932 sq. ft
Boiler pressure, 120 lbs per sq. in.
Capacity, water, 820 gallons; coal, 47.5 cu. ft
Weight in working order, 30 tons 8 cwt

A fourth locomotive, an exact copy of the other three, the *Ventnor* (Makers' No. 848) was bought in 1868.

These locomotives had extremely tall copper-topped chimneys which were soon shortened, though the copper caps were retained, and no cabs when first delivered, the men finding what protection they could behind a small weather board.

The original appearance of these engines can be seen in the photograph of the *Ryde*, taken in 1864, on page 28.

With their original boilers, the dome, with a polished brass casing, was situated over the fire box and the nearness of the spring balance safety valves must have suggested an easy way of obtaining an extra 5 lbs of pressure for the ascent of Apse.

Cabs were added to these engines and hand rails placed on top of the tanks to enable the men to go to the front of the engine while in motion.

When these four locomotives were reboilered, which took place about 1896, the dome was placed in the middle of the boiler barrel while the *Ryde* was alone in having a second dome and safety valve of polished brass and copper over the firebox, the others having a manhole cover and whistle.

The next addition to the Isle of Wight Railway stock was the *Wroxall* from the same makers, Works No. 1141, which arrived in 1872.

The *Wroxall* was not sensibly different from her four predecessors, though she arrived with the dome in the middle of the boiler, a cab, and injectors in place of pumps. The hand rails were added later.

There were a few trifling dimensional differences, a slightly smaller heating surface of 927 sq. ft against 932, and coal capacity of 48 cu. ft as opposed to 47.5, an increase in wheel diameter of ½ inch, and an increase in weight of 24 cwt.

In 1879 a further engine arrived from Beyer, Peacock & Co. (Works No. 1638), and was named *Brading*; she was similar in appearance to the others, but a more powerful machine.

The dimensions of this enlarged engine were:

Cylinders (inside), 16 inches by 24 inches
Wheels, coupled, 5 feet ½ inch; leading, 3 feet 6½ inches
Heating surface, 960.8 sq. ft
Boiler pressure, 120 lbs per sq. in
Capacity, water, 1,000 gallons; coal, 50 cu. ft
Weight in working order, 34 tons 8 cwt

In 1882 another engine was acquired, this time a 0-6-0 saddle tank built in 1875 by Manning, Wardle & Co., of Leeds (Works No. 517) for the contractor making the Brading Harbour branch; this engine was taken over when the IWR started to work the branch.

The engine was used almost entirely on the branch line and was named *Bembridge*. The leading features were:

Cylinders (inside), 13 inches by 18 inches
Wheels, 3 feet
Heating surface, 540 sq. ft
Boiler pressure, 120 lbs per sq. in.
Capacity, water, 500 gallons; coal, 46 cu. ft

About 1910 slight alterations were made to the engine including the replacement of the copper-capped chimney by one of the stovepipe variety.

The *Bembridge* was bought by the Government for War service abroad, and left the Island, never to return, in 1917.

The last addition to the IWR was the *Bonchurch*, a 2-4-0 tank of the type of the others but much more powerful; she was built by Beyer, Peacock & Co. (Makers' No. 2376) in 1883, and had the following particulars:

Cylinders (inside) 17 inches by 24 inches
Wheels, driving, 5 feet ½ inch; leading, 3 feet 6½ inches
Heating surface, 950.5 sq. ft
Boiler pressure, 120 lbs sq. in.
Capacity, Water, 1,000 gallons; coal, 77 cu. ft
Weight in working order, 35 tons 14 cwt

The *Bonchurch* differed somewhat markedly in appearance from the others as the bunker was placed outside the cab while a round topped dome was situated on the boiler with Ramsbottom safety valves on the fire box. This engine had a misfortune on arrival in the Island as the lighter conveying her rolled, whereupon the *Bonchurch* fell into the sea at St Helen's where she remained for some days!

Until a few years before the War the IWR engines presented a very ornate appearance with copper chimney tops, and polished brass domes with bell mouths; the colour of the locomotives was then a much darker red than later, almost chocolate, but from about 1910 the livery has undergone change.

The copper chimney caps were then replaced by cast-iron tops of a rather pleasing design which was altered in 1920, a new type of standard chimney, shorter and uglier, making its appearance then, the *Ryde* being the first engine so fitted.

The tank rails and bell mouths of the domes were discarded with the chimney caps and the domes were all painted over except in the case of the *Bonchurch* which retained the polished brass until 1921. The second dome of the *Ryde* was also removed before the War.

The red colour of the engines became lighter until it was definitely Midland red.

The spring balances of the various engines were arranged somewhat differently; on the *Ryde* and the *Ventnor* they were side by side close together, while the *Sandown*, *Shanklin*, *Wroxall*, and *Brading* had them spread wide apart at an angle of about 30 degrees. During their last overhauls before amalgamation these positions were reversed respecting the *Ryde* and *Shanklin* so that now the spring balances are splayed out on the former and side by side on the latter.

The first five of the Beyer & Peacock tanks had three circular windows in the back of the cab while *Brading* and *Bonchurch* had two rectangular ones.

Locomotives on this section always run bunker first towards Ryde.

The whistles of the IWR were very characteristic as they had a high piercing note, offering a great contrast with the hooters of the Central engines.

Left: Isle of Wight Railway locomotive, *Brading*.

Below: Bonchurch, IWR at Sandown.

The Freshwater, Yarmouth & Newport Railway

When this Railway decided to fend for itself in 1913 it purchased two tank engines. No. 1 was a 0-6-0 inside cylinder saddle tank built by Manning, Wardle & Co., of Leeds (Works No. 1555) in 1902 and had the following dimensions:

Cylinders (inside) 14 inches by 20 inches
Wheels, 3 feet 6 inches
Heating surface, 688.5 sq. ft
Boiler pressure, 140 lbs per sq. in.
Capacity, water, 600 gallons; coal, 47 cu. ft
Weight in working order, 27 tons

The locomotive was painted green and lettered 'F.Y. & N. Rly'.

No. 2 is an engine with an interesting history; it was one of the Stroudley 'Terriers' and was No. 46, *Newington* on the London, Brighton & South Coast Railway, being built in 1876.

It was sold to the LSWR in March, 1903, who used it on the Lyme Regis branch, numbering it 734. The South Western retained the copper-capped chimney but reboilered it and fitted it with Drummond type safety valves. In June, 1913, it was sold to the F.Y.N.R. and ran for a long time on this system in the LSWR colours. It was eventually repainted bright green with red connecting rods, and lettered FYN.

In addition to these locomotives, a 20-hp Drewry petrol rail-motor to seat 12 was obtained by the railway.

The rail-motor was of interest as it ran the only regular non-stop service in the Island, from Freshwater to Newport with a stop at Yarmouth. This service was in the nature of a boat train as it was 'limited' to mainland passengers only.

Apart from the locomotives actually owned by the Island Railways, certain contractors' engines ran in the Isle of Wight at various times, such as the *Pioneer* and *Precursor* of the Newport & Cowes line and the *Bembridge* of the Isle of Wight Railway. In addition to these there were two six-coupled tanks named *St. Helen's* and *Godshill* which left the Island when constructional work was completed; the former was used in building the Brading Harbour branch and the latter on the Newport, Godshill & St Lawrence Railway.

About the *Godshill* a good story is told; this locomotive, if it needed repairs, was sent to the Ryde works of the Isle of Wight Railway, the repairs being paid for by the contractor building the Newport, Godshill & St Lawrence line. On one occasion, however, the money for the repairs was not immediately forthcoming, so that the Isle of Wight Railway, who did business on a cash down basis, ordered the locomotive to be secured to the rails of the repair shop with chains to guard against its surreptitious removal, while a man was detailed to watch night and day in the shop.

The man had to wait a fortnight until the money was found and the IWR released their security against a bad debt.

5

Locomotives since Amalgamation

The moment the Southern Railway was established in the Island, it began to set its locomotive house in order.

Early in 1923 two 0-4-4 Adams tanks from the LSWR were shipped across, still in their LSWR livery, to offer some relief for the IWR main line services for that summer. These two engines were numbered 206 and 211 and were landed at Ryde Pier Head station, with some additional coaching stock by means of an Admiralty floating crane and were shedded at Ryde. Later, the Southern Railway purchased one for themselves and from then landed locomotives and stock at Medina Wharf.

As soon as the arrival of the new tanks made it possible to dispense with an engine, the *Sandown* of the Isle of Wight Railway, which had been working the Brading Harbour branch (the duty of the engine longest without a refit), was removed to Eastleigh for scrapping as she was found to have a cracked frame and to be in bad repair generally, so that she was not worth the expense of a heavy overhaul.

The Island locomotives and engines sent over from the Mainland were not numbered in any of the three series that were used for the Mainland groups of the Southern Railway, but formed a separate group of their own having the prefix W; the IWCR and FYNR engines retained their old numbers, while the IWR locomotives which had never before been numbered were included in the series with numbers 13 to 18, retaining their names.

The two Adams tanks, 206 and 211, later became Nos W19 and W20, while further Adams tanks already numbered in the Island scheme from W21 to W31, were shipped over in pairs at various dates, mentioned later. The LSWR tank No. W25 and all engines coming over or being repainted subsequent to W25's arrival, appeared in the new standard livery of the Southern Railway, a dark apple-green, whereas the previous standard colour had been a sage-green shade.

The Adams tanks W27 to W31 inclusive are fitted with the Drummond type dome and safety valves, while engines arriving before these had the Adams type dome and a safety valve over the firebox. As the vacuum brake is the standard on the LSWR, the Adams tanks were all fitted with the Westinghouse brake before despatch, the reservoir being placed over the tank on the left hand side.

No. W21, an Adams Tank at work on the Island.

W28, one of the last Adams Tanks on the Island.

W15 *Ventnor* on a Sandown train at Newport.

The leading dimensions of the Adams tanks are as follows:

Cylinders (inside), 17½ inches by 24 inches
Wheels, coupled, 4 feet 10 inches; trailing, 3 feet
Heating surface, 987 sq. ft
Boiler pressure, 160 lbs per sq. in.
Capacity, water, 800 gallons; coal, 1½ tons
Weight in working order, 46 tons 18 cwt

An additional 'Terrier', which was given the number of W3, was transported to the Island in 1927 to replace W9, ex No. 9 of the Isle of Wight Central Railway that had been damaged and was not worth repair; this engine was numbered 677 in the books of the London, Brighton & South Coast Railway but had been previously No. 77 *Wonersh*.

W3 has the enlarged bunker found on the 'Terriers' in the Island and a slightly extended smokebox but retains the old boiler and the original copper-capped chimney painted over.

Repainting of the Island locomotives proceeded apace, the first to appear in the Southern sage-green being Nos 8 and 11 of the IWCR and No. 2 of the FYNR, followed shortly by *Ventnor* of the IWR. The only Island engines that did not assume the new colours were Nos 4, 6, and 7 of the IWC and *Sandown* of the IWR, though No. 6 acquired a Southern Railway green number plate for the back of the bunker. All the other Island engines appeared in the unfamiliar green, while No. 11, the Central 'Terrier', and the *Ryde* have been repainted twice and are now in the dark apple-green.

Both the Freshwater engines have been retained in service; No. 1, which by the way is the most modern engine in the Island, is proving very useful as a shunting tank at Medina Wharf as she has a high tractive output, while No. 2 is used as a branch line engine.

The latter has been fitted with a Westinghouse brake to enable her to run with Mainland stock, while the bunker has been enlarged and the copper-capped chimney painted over.

The ranks of the Central engines, however, have been very much thinned as these locomotives developed minor defects and were, in general, of insufficient power to be worth an expensive refit, so that they were sent to the scrap heap as soon as enough Adams tanks had arrived to replace them. Nos 4, 6 and 7, which retained their sombre black until the end, were among the first to go, while Nos 5 and 9, which were repainted, have also been scrapped; the former, having been overhauled at Ryde, worked the Brading Harbour branch for some time.

All the old Isle of Wight Railway engines suffered from the same complaint, cracked trailing-axle frames, and, as has been said, this caused the immediate removal of the *Sandown*; with the other engines, however, repairs were made to keep them on the road until they could be relieved.

To this end, the cracks on the *Bonchurch*, the most powerful and therefore the most useful engine of the class, were electrically welded, while the others were satisfactorily patched up. As soon as possible, however, the *Ventnor* and *Brading* were sent to join the *Sandown* on the scrap heap, while the *Shanklin* was sold in November, 1927, and at the end of the year was lying dead waiting to be broken up.

In addition to the *Bonchurch*, the *Ryde* and *Wroxall* are still in good condition and will, it is to be hoped, give good service for many years to come.

The *Ryde* has, unfortunately, lost many of her good looks by the unhappy addition of a South Western pattern chimney, which looks most out of place on an Isle of Wight engine.

The following list gives particulars of arrivals and removals of locomotives:

Old No	Railway	Date built	Type	New No.	Remarks
No. 1	FYN	1902	0-6-0	W1	
No. 2	"	1876	"	W2	
No. 677	LBSC		"	W3	Sent June, 1927
No. 4	IWC	1876	2-4-0	W4	Scrapped July 1925
No. 5	"	"	"	W5	Scrapped Aug 1926
No. 6	"	1890	4-4-0	W6	Scrapped March 1926
No. 7	"	1882	2-4-0	W7	Scrapped July 1926
No. 8	"	1898	"	W8	
No. 9	"	1872	0-6-0	W9	Scrapped May 1927
No. 10	"	1874	"	W10	
No. 11	"	1878	"	W11	
No. 12	"	1880	"	W12	
Ryde	IWR	1864	2-4-0	W13	
Sandown	"	"	"	–	Scrapped June 1923
Shanklin	"	"	"	W14	Sold Nov 1927
Ventnor	"	1868	"	W15	Scrapped July 1925
Wroxall	"	1872	"	W16	
Brading	"	1879	"	W17	Scrapped July 1926.
Bonchurch	"	1883	"	W18	
No. 206	LSWR	1891	0-4-4	W19	Sent May 1923
No. 211	"	"	"	W20	Sent May 1923
No. 205	"	"	"	W21	Sent June 1924
No. 215	"	1892	"	W22	Sent June 1924
No. 188	"	1890	"	W23	Sent April 1925
No. 209	"	1891	"	W24	Sent April 1925
No. 190	"	1890	"	W25	Sent June 1925
No. 210	"	1891	"	W26	Sent June 1925
No. 184	"	1890	"	W27	Sent March 1926
No. 186	"	"	"	W28	Sent March 1926
No. 202	"	1891	"	W29	Sent April 1926
No. 219	"	1892	"	W30	Sent April 1926
No. 180	"	1890	"	W31	Sent May 1927

As regards locomotive duties, the distribution of engines in the summer of 1927 will give an idea of the manner in which they are performed. Of the thirteen Adams tanks, seven were shedded at Ryde for the IWR main line while six were kept at Newport for the Cowes–Ryde and Cowes–Sandown services; all the 'Terriers' were kept at Newport and were used on the Freshwater and Ventnor West branches and for shunting duties generally. In addition No. W18, *Bonchurch*, and W1 were at Newport for goods train work.

Right: W15 *Ventnor* on Sandown train at Newport.

Left: The *Brading* in Southern Railway colours.

Right: Double-headed goods train at Newport with W12 and W8.

The three remaining IWR tanks *Ryde*, *Shanklin* and *Wroxall* were all shedded at Ryde and took it in turns to work the Brading Harbour branch as they were no longer required for main line work after the summer of 1926. The only other engine is No. W8 which is kept in reserve either at Newport or Ryde.

The following is a table showing locomotive strengths in the Island at various times.

Date	IWCR	IWR	FYNR	SR Importations	Total
1887	7	8	–	–	15
1914	12	8	2	–	22
31 Dec 1922	9	7	2	–	18
31 Dec 1923	9	6	2	2	19
30 June 1925	9	6	2	8	25
31 Dec 1926	5	4	2	12	23
31 Dec 1927	4	3	2	14	23

The tunnel and signal box at Ventnor station. Note the SR on the open top wagon *(CMcC)*

IoW Railways Update

P. C. Allen's account, *The Railways of the Isle of Wight*, was published in 1928 at a time when the Southern Railway ran the Island's trains. Apart from some changes to the track layout, such as the installation of double track from Brading to Sandown and new passing loops at Smallbrook Junction, it remained much as it had been. The other innovation under the SR was the introduction of the Island's only named train, *The Tourist*, which ran from Ventnor to Freshwater via Sandown, Merston and Newport.

1948 saw the nationalisation of Britain's railways and over the ensuing decades a programme of 'modernisation' saw the lines closed one after the other. The former Freshwater, Yarmouth & Newport Railway (FYNR) line, the Ventnor West line, Bembridge branch and Sandown to Newport line had closed by the end of 1956. The line between Smallbrook Junction and Cowes survived the initial wave of closures in the 1950s but with the end of steam on the horizon the reprieve was short lived with the line closing to passengers under the Beeching cuts in February 1966. Goods traffic continued to Cowes and Newport for a few months but that too was withdrawn by May 1966. Also in 1966, Dr Beeching's axe threatened to fall. Ten years later, in 1966, Dr Beeching's axe threatened to fall on the 8½-mile line between Ryde and Shanklin, but was electrified instead using the third rail system, and from March 1967 it was worked with ex-London Underground stock (originally London Electric Railway stock built between 1923-31), Class 485 and 486 trains. (ex-London Underground 1938-built tube stock.) Branded as the Island Line it was privatised in 1996 and was later absorbed into the South Western franchise although the electric services continue to operate under as Island Line Trains. The trains connect with ferries arriving from Portsmouth at Ryde Pier head, giving rise to the unexpected sight of Underground-style trains on the pier itself.

In 1971 the Isle of Wight Railway Co. Ltd was formed to purchase a short section of line between Wootton and Havenstreet. Over the years this has been extended from Havenstreet towards Ryde to eventually reach the Smallbrook Junction on the Ryde–Shanklin line, where a new station was constructed enabling passengers to transfer to and from the Island Line trains. Further extensions have been proposed. The most likely would be westwards from Wootton to Newport, although building on parts of the old line may limit this to the outskirts of Newport. Another possibility is an extension from Smallbrook Junction to Ryde St John's Road station using one of the two Island Line tracks on this stretch of line.

The Photographs

The following collection of images is divided into seven sections:

- Pre-nationalisation
- Post-nationalisation
- Preserved Steam
- Locations
- Diesel Shunters
- The Island Line and Ryde Pier
- Railway Company Ferries

Sources are acknowledged individually on the captions and collectively on page 95.

This page: Early morning mist with 24 *Calbourne* well into its stride between Smallbrook Junction and Ashey in 2010. *(Gordon Edgar)*

Pre-nationalisation

Above: Sandown, a 2-4-0 built for the IWR in 1864. Scrapped June 1923.

Below: IWC No. 9, coupled 0-6-0, built in 1872, scrapped in May 1927. *(Both CMcC)*

W32 coming into Newport in April 1937. *(CMcC)*

Above: Unidentified 4-4-0, photographed in the 1930s.

Below: IWC No. 12, built in 1880 and later renumbered as W12. *(Both CMcC)*

Above: W8 photographed in 1937. As No. 8 it was built in 1898 for the IWC. *(CMcC)*

Opposite top: W22, formerly No. 215 of the LSWR, pulling into Ventnor station.

Opposite bottom: Southern Railway No. 4 at Newport. *(Both CMcC)*

Southern Railway No. 22 at Ventnor station. *(CMcC)*

Sandown – see page 49 for side view. *(CMcC)*

W14 in Southern Railway colours, at Ventnor, with the tunnel and signal box in the background. *(CMcC)*

Post-nationalisation

24 *Calbourne* at Ryde shed in the summer of 1964. (Gordon Edgar/A. E. Durrant/Gordon Edgar Collection)

18, *Ningwood*, at Ryde (70H) shed in the summer of 1964. This locomotive was withdrawn from service in December the following year. (Gordon Edgar/A. E. Durrant/Gordon Edgar Collection)

Above: 31, *Chale*, at Shanklin on 15 May 1956.

Opposite top: 20, *Shanklin*, starts away from Ryde St John's with a service to Ventnor in 1964.

Opposite bottom: 21, *Sandown*, runs into Shanklin from Ventnor while 26, *Whitwell*, waits to depart for Ventnor during 1963.

(All images Gordon Edgar/ A. E. Durrant/Gordon Edgar Collection)

22, *Brading*, heading for Ventnor, seen in the cutting on the steep climb at Wroxall in the summer of 1964. *(Gordon Edgar/A. E. Durrant/Gordon Edgar Collection)*

28, Ashey, at Ventnor on 17 May 1956. *(Gordon Edgar/A. E. Durrant/Gordon Edgar Collection)*

Preserved Steam

Above: Saddle Tank 198 seen at Smallbrook Junction in 2012. *(Peter Trimming)*

Opposite top: 17, *Seaview*, runs into Cowes station with a service from Ryde, shortly before withdrawal of passenger services and closure of the line. *(Gordon Edgar Collection)*

Opposite bottom: 28, *Ashey*, departing from Ryde St John's with a service for Ventnor in the summer of 1964. *(Both Gordon Edgar/A. E. Durrant/Gordon Edgar Collection)*

Above: 24, *Calbourne*, in black with British Railways' 'rocking horse' emblem. *(Gary Ashanollah/busman1982)*

Opposite top: LBSCR Stroudley 'A1X, 0-6-0T. It was numbered by the LBSCR as No.40, and by the Southern Railway (IoW section) as W11, Newport with SR No. 2640, changed to BR No. 32640 at Haven Street, Isle of Wight Railway, in 2000.

Opposite bottom: LSWR Adams Class 'O2' 0-4-4T, SR (IoW section) W24. Originally LSWR No. 209 *Calbourne*, then SR No. E209. In 1925 Maunsell Parson's Green livery at Haven Street.

(Both photographs Hugh Llewelyn)

Locations

Above: Royal Engineer taking on water at Haven Street, 2012. *(Peter Trimming)*

Below: LBSCR Brake Third No. S2416, photographed with some SECR coaches at Haven Street in 2000. *(Hugh Llewelyn)*

Above: Level crossing at Haven Street station, in 2012. *(Peter Trimming)*

Below: Sandown station in 2007. *(Bashereyre)*

Above: Platform at Wootton station.
(A1personage)

Right: The forecourt of Shanklin
station. Opened in 1864, it now
serves the Island Line. *(Bashereyre)*

Diesel Shunters

Army 235, Andrew Barclay 0-4-0 diesel W/No. 371, 1945 and Army 230, Vulcan Foundry W/No. 5265, Drewry Car Co. W/No. 2184 built 1945, inside the shed at MoD Moreton-on-Lugg on 14 December 1985. '235' was donated to the Isle of Wight Steam Railway. *(Gordon Edgar)*

Above: Ex-BR class 05 Hunslet 0-6-0 diesel shunter, W/No. 4870, built in 1956 and photographed at the Haven Street yard in November 2010.

Right: Class 03 No. 03079 outside Ryde St John's depot and works in July 1985.

Below: Another view of Army 235, the wartime-designed 0-4-0 diesel. After a spell at the National Army Museum at Beverley, upon closure it was donated to the IoW Steam Railway. *(Gordon Edgar)*

The Island Line and Ryde Pier

24 *Calbourne* heading a train away from Ryde Pier Head station and approaching Ryde Esplanade on 15 May 1956. *(Gordon Edgar/Gordon Edgar Collection)*

Above: View across the esplanade at Ryde with the tracks disappearing below ground to enter the tunnel, *c.* 1900. *(LoC)*

Below: A 2009 view of this section, which is now part of the Island Line. *(Editor5807)*

The ex-Southern Railway Baguley/Drewry Car Company tram, built in 1927, and shown working a shuttle service on Ryde Pier in May 1956. (*Gordon Edgar/Gordon Edgar Collection*)

33, *Bembridge*, on the pier at Ryde on 15 May 1956. *(Gordon Edgar/Gordon Edgar Collection)*

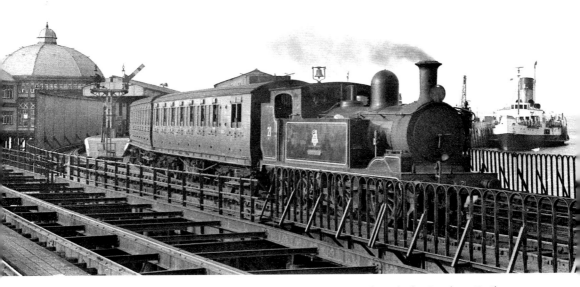

Above: 21, *Sandown*, stands at Ryde Pier Head station approach with the Southern Railway paddle steamer *Sandown* berthed on the jetty behind. For more railway-company-operated steamers to the Island, see page 90. *(Gordon Edgar/Gordon Edgar Collection)*

Below: Unit No. 485 045 leading a Shanklin train at Ryde St John's Road, with 03079 stabled on shed, 9 July 1985. *(Gordon Edgar)*

An Island Line train of ex-London Underground 1938 stock on Ryde Pier, heading towards the Ryde esplanade. Photographed in March 2010. *(Editor5807)*

Above: 486 034 and hybrid unit 485 044 pause at Ryde St John's Road, forming a Shanklin–Ryde Pier Head service on 9 July 1985.

Below: 485044 leading at Ryde St John's Road on the same day. *(Gordon Edgar)*

An evening service from Shanklin to Ryde Pier Head on 15 November 2010. It is pausing at the former Isle of Wight Central Railway station at Ryde St John's Road. Note the ornate ironwork on the canopy, which incorporates the railway company's monogram. *(Gordon Edgar)*

Ryde St John's Road in the daylight, with Island Line Class 483, No. 004, in its deep red London Underground livery. *(Peter Skuse)*

Above: The driver of unit 486 034 takes a break while waiting for a clear line to Shanklin, at Sandown station, Isle of Wight, July 1985.

Below: Unit 486 034 forming a Shanklin–Ryde service at Brading, still with working gas lamps. Photographed in July 1985. *(Both Gordon Edgar)*

The 08.38 Shanklin–Ryde Pier Head Island Line service has no passengers to board and is ready to depart from a much rationalised Brading station on 17 November 2010. The whole of the station complex and signal box is now Grade II listed. *(Gordon Edgar)*

Island Line Class 483 No. 004, at a sunny Shanklin station. *(Peter Skuse)*

Above: With Shanklin and the Down in the distance, the 09.18 Shanklin–Ryde Pier Head service passes Marshcomb Copse at Yarbridge near Brading on 17 November 2010.

Below: Shanklin and Ryde services cross at Ryde St John's Road station in June 1977. *(Gordon Edgar Collection)*

A Shanklin train arrives at Smallbrook Junction, March 2012. *(Peter Trimming)*

Above: Train on Ryde Pier, photographed in October 2011. *(Phil Sangwell)*

Below: Summer 1971, this Ryde Pier Head–Ryde Esplanade shuttle is formed of unit 485 043, which was also fitted with de-icing equipment for winter third rail ice clearance use. *(Gordon Edgar Collection)*

Above: A colourful livery for this Class 483 on the Island Line. Photographed in 2006.
(A1personage)

Opposite: A popular train for commuters, the 07.18 Island Lines Trains' Shanklin–Ryde Pier Head for connection with the ferry for Portsmouth rumbles across the pier on 15 November 2010. Ryde Pier was in fact three piers, with the promenade pier for pedestrians and vehicles, built in 1840 and enlarged a number of times; a tramway pier built in 1864, which for many years took passengers to catch the ferry; and a railway pier built in 1880. The latter is still in use and was electrified in 1967. The tramway pier, operated at one time by a Baguley/Drewry-built railcar – see page 73 – is the middle of the three but is no longer in use and has been partially dismantled. Ryde Pier is the longest in England after Southend Pier, and at 2,250 feet it is almost ½ mile in length. At one time there was an entertainment complex at the pier head including a theatre and a bar, but these fell into disuse and have been demolished. *(Gordon Edgar)*

Dinosaurs in 2007. *(Bashereyre)*

Railway Company Ferries

By 1880, the LSWR and LBSCR had created a joint company to operate steamers to the Isle of Wight. It operated from the harbour at Portsmouth and from Ryde Pier. Known as the South Western and Brighton Railway Companies Steam Packet Service, it was eventually amalgamated into the Southern Railway in 1923. Both the Southern and British Railways operated to the Island, too, with the BR Sealink service eventually becoming the privately owned Wightlink. Other companies, operating both ferry services and pleasure sailings, included P&A Campbell (with their White Funnel fleet), Cosens of Weymouth, and the Red Funnel service, which still operates today from Southampton to Cowes.

The Cosens paddle steamer *Monarch* at Ryde Pier in the 1920s. *Monarch* was built at Blackwall, London, in 1888. She spent much of her later life on the Bournemouth–Swanage service. *(CMcC)*

The *Shanklin* was built in Southampton in 1924 as one of the first new paddlers of the Southern Railway. She lasted through the Second World War, when she remained on the Isle of Wight service, and was finally scrapped in 1961 at Cork. *(CMcC)*

The Southern Railway's *Southsea* was the sister ship to the *Whippingham* and was built in 1930 at the Fairfield yard in Govan, now BAE Systems. She had a short career, being lost off the Tyne in 1941 when minesweeping the entrance to the river. *(CMcC)*

Above: Whippingham was often used for excursions in pre-war days. Laid up at the start of the war, she evacuated 2,700 from Dunkirk's beaches in 1940. *Whippingham* spent the days prior to D-Day loading soldiers onto ships at Spithead. Her last voyage was to Ghent, Belgium, for scrapping in 1963. *(CMcC)*

Below: The Duchess of Fife was built in 1899 and lasted until 1929. This view dates from around 1904 and shows her leaving Ryde Pier. *(CMcC)*

Cosens' *Bournemouth Queen* and one of the Southern Railway steamers leave Ryde Pier in the 1930s. Paddle steamers were used for their manoeuvrability and ability to turn around quickly at the piers. By the post-war period, they would begin to be replaced by motor vessels, often much more economic and easier to operate with fewer crew. *(CMcC)*

Bibliography

Bibliography from the 1928 Edition

'Multum in Parvo', by C. L. Conacher, in the *Railway Magazine, March*, 1899.

Interview with C. L. Conacher, in the *Railway Magazine, January*, 1908.

'The Freshwater, Yarmouth & Newport Railway', by H. S. G. Eastman, in the *Railway Magazine, June*, 1914.

'The Railways of the Isle of Wight', by H. M. Alderman, in the *Railway Magazine, July*, 1914.

'The Isle of Wight and the Southern Railway', by G. W. Tripp, in the *Railway Magazine, April*, 1924.

'The Locomotive History of the Isle of Wight Central Railway', by W. V. Cauchi, in the *Locomotive, November*, 1900, *January, February*, and *March*, 1901.

'The Isle of Wight Railway and Its Locomotives', by A. R. Bennett, in the *Locomotive, September* and *October*, 1920.

'The Locomotives of the Isle of Wight Central Railway', in the *Locomotive, December*, 1921.

'The Railways of the Isle of Wight', by G. G. Jackson, in the *Railway and Travel Monthly, April* and *May*, 1919.

'The Railways of the Isle of Wight', by C. N. A., in the *Southern Railway Magazine, June*, 1926.

The Locomotives of the Railways of the Isle of Wight, by P. C. Walker, 1920.

The Railway Year Book.

New Bibliography

A number of very useful books on the Island's railways have been published in recent years:

Isle of Wight Lines – 50 Years of Change, Vic Mitchell & Keith Smith, Middleton Press, 1998.

Railways of the Isle of Wight, Marie Panter, Stenlake Publishing, 2013.

Steaming Through the Isle of Wight, Peter Hay, Middleton Press, 1988.

The Isle of Wight Railway, R. J. Maycock & R. Silsbury, The Oakwood Press, 1999.

The Isle of Wight Railways – From 1923 Onwards, R. J. Maycock & R. Silsbury, The Oakwood Press, 2006.

Vectis Steam – The Last Years of the Isle of Wight Railway, Laurie Golden, Ian Allan, 2011.

Calbourne on the curve near Ashey station, 16 November 2010. *(Gordon Edgar)*

Acknowledgements

As stated, the majority of the early images within the main text have come from the 1928 edition of P. C. Allen's book. Additional photographs are individually credited on the captions, and for permission to use them I am grateful in particular to Campbell McCutcheon (CMcC) and Gordon Edgar for providing the lion's share; my thanks also go to NASA, the US Library of Congress (LoC), Peter Trimming, Gary Ashanollah/ busman1982, Bashereyre, A1personage, Editor5897, Peter Skuse and Phil Sangwell.

Also available from Amberley Publishing

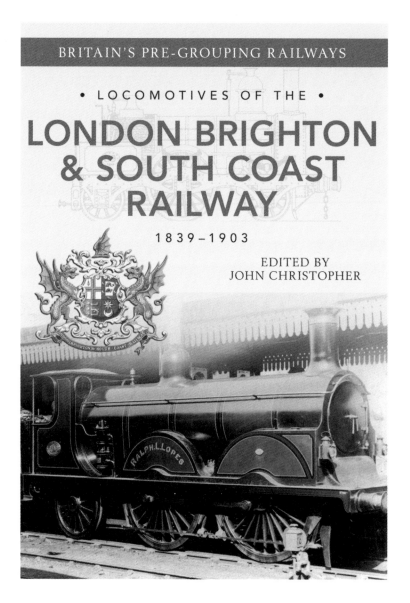

BRITAIN'S PRE-GROUPING RAILWAYS

• LOCOMOTIVES OF THE •

LONDON BRIGHTON & SOUTH COAST RAILWAY

1839–1903

EDITED BY
JOHN CHRISTOPHER